Timeless Motivational Quotes

A Treasury of Inspiration Through the Ages

Quotes Book 1

Alexander Mindset

Copyright © 2024
All rights reserved.

Table of Contens

Introduction	5
How to Use Quotes as a Daily Source of Encouragement and Strength	7
Positive quotes for motivation	10
Positive Quotes for Brightening Your Day	20
Positive Quotes for Improving Your Mindset	24
Positive Quotes for Making Days Better	33
Positive Thinking Quotes for Overcoming Challenges	41
Mood-Boosting Inspirational Quotes	49
Self-Esteem Enhancing Motivational Quotes	58
Optimism-Building Positive Quotes	64
Deep motivational quotes	70
Motivational quotes about success	77
Motivational quotes for personal life	87
Motivational quotes for work	94
Motivational quotes for women	100
Motivational quotes for men	115
Positive Thinking Quotes For Kids	123
Motivational quotes for students	134
Success quotes	139
Funny motivational quotes	151
Short motivational quotes	166
Motivational Monday quotes	176
Friday motivational quotes	184
Best motivational quotes to start your day	189
Daily motivational quotes	196
Inspirational quotes	208
Positive quotes	219
Encouraging quotes	224
Motivation quotes	231
Quotes about life	239
More motivating quotes	249
Inspirational quotes for the new year	263

> **"**
> # It always seems impossible until it's done.
>
> *Nelson Mandela*

Introduction

Dear Reader,

Welcome to a world of inspiration, wisdom, and power encapsulated in words. Before you is not just a collection of quotes, but a true treasure trove of ideas capable of transforming your life. In our rapidly changing world, full of challenges and uncertainty, we often need a source of stability and inspiration. Carefully selected quotes from outstanding individuals can become such a source.

Why are quotes so important? They represent the quintessence of human experience and wisdom expressed in a concise, memorable form. It's as if you could instantly access the deepest insights of history's greatest minds. Quotes are capable of:

1. Inspiring and motivating when you feel your strength is running out.
2. Offering new perspectives in difficult situations.
3. Comforting and supporting in tough times.
4. Encouraging action and personal growth.
5. Reminding us of important life truths that we tend to foget in the bustle of everyday life.

Incorporating quotes into your daily routine can become a powerful tool for transformation. Imagine starting each morning with a thought that sets the tone for the entire day. Or having a reliable source of wisdom to turn to in moments of doubt. Regular interaction with inspiring quotes can gradually change your mindset, make you more resilient to stress, and open to new opportunities.

In this book, we have collected quotes for all of life's occasions: from overcoming difficulties to achieving success, from finding happiness to attaining inner peace. Each section is carefully compiled to address various needs and situations you may encounter.

We invite you not just to read these quotes, but to actively engage with them. Reflect on their meaning, apply their wisdom in your life, share them with others. Let them become your companions, advisors, and sources of inspiration.

Remember, the power of a quote is revealed not in the moment of reading it, but in the instant you begin to live according to its message. May this book become not just a collection of beautiful phrases, but a guide to action, a catalyst for positive changes in your life.

Discover the power of words. Let the wisdom of ages inspire you every day. Welcome to the journey towards the best version of yourself!

> **Don't watch the clock; do what it does. Keep going.**
>
> *Sam Levenson*

How to Use Quotes as a Daily Source of Encouragement and Strength

Here's how you can effectively use this book tof enrich your everyday life:

Daily Reflection Practice

Open a new page of the book each morning. One quote per day is the ideal amount for deep contemplation. Read the quote aloud, then close your eyes and let its meaning sink into your consciousness.

If you come across a quote that seemingly doesn't relate to you directly (for example, if you're a woman and the quote appears to be for men), don't skip it. Instead, challenge yourself to work with it. Try to apply it to your own life and uncover its deeper, universal meaning. Often, the quotes that seem least relevant at first glance can offer the most profound insights when we approach them with an open mind.

Keeping a Reflection Journal

Use the space under the quote to write down your thoughts, associations, and ideas. This is not just note-taking - it's your personal dialogue with the wisdom of ages. Ask yourself:

- How does this quote relate to my life today?
- What actions can I take based on this wisdom?
- How can this thought change my approach to current challenges?

Setting an Intention for the Day

Based on the quote and your reflections, formulate an intention for the day. This can be a specific action or a general mindset. Write it down under your reflections.

Visual Reminder

Take a photo of the quote of the day and set it as the background image on your phone or computer. This will serve as a constant reminder of your intention throughout the day.

Evening Reflection

Before bed, return to the quote of the day. Reflect on how it manifested in your day. Write down any new thoughts or observations.

Weekly Review

At the end of the week, review all the quotes and your notes from the past days. Note any patterns or insights. This will help you track your progress and more deeply integrate the wisdom gained.

Sharing Thoughts

Share the quote of the day with a friend or family member. Discuss what it means to each of you. This will not only enrich your understanding but also strengthen your relationships.

Creative Expression

Once a week, choose a quote that particularly resonated with you and express its meaning creatively - draw, write a poem, or create a collage. This will help you internalize its message more deeply.

Meditating on the Quote

Set aside 5-10 minutes for meditation, focusing on the quote of the day. Allow its meaning to penetrate your subconscious.

Real-Life Application

Challenge yourself to apply the wisdom of the quote in a specific life situation. In the evening, write down how this influenced your actions and their results.

Remember, the power of this practice lies not in the number of quotes read, but in the depth of your interaction with each one. One thoughtfully lived idea can change your day, week, or even life. Let each page of this book become a step on the path to a better version of yourself.

May this journey be filled with discoveries, growth, and inspiration!

> Don't look at your feet to see if you are doing it right. Just dance.

Anne Lamott

> Someone's sitting in the shade today because someone planted a tree a long time ago.

Warren Buffet

> True freedom is impossible without a mind made free by discipline.

Mortimer J. Adler

> Rivers know this: there is no hurry. We shall get there someday.

A. A. Milne

> There is a vitality, a life force, an energy, a quickening that is translated through you into action, and because there is only one of you in all time, this expression is unique. And if you block it, it will never exist through any other medium and will be lost.

Martha Graham

> Small is not just a stepping stone. Small is a great destination itself.

Jason Fried

> He that can have patience can have what he will.

Benjamin Franklin

> The only one who can tell you 'you can't win' is you, and you don't have to listen.

Jessica Ennis

> Set your goals high, and don't stop till you get there.

Bo Jackson

> Take your victories, whatever they may be, cherish them, use them, but don't settle for them.

Mia Hamm

> The way I see it, if you want the rainbow, you gotta put up with the rain!

Dolly Parton

> We cannot direct the wind, but we can adjust the sails.

Dolly Parton

> Be so happy that, when other people look at you, they become happy too.

Anonymous

> Be the change that you wish to see in the world.

Mahatma Gandhi

> Nothing is impossible, the word itself says 'I'm possible.'

Audrey Hepburn

> The most important thing is to try and inspire people so that they can be great in whatever they want to do.

Kobe Bryant

"

It's your outlook on life that counts. If you take yourself lightly and don't take yourself too seriously, pretty soon you can find the humor in our everyday lives. And sometimes it can be a lifesaver.

Betty White

> Once you replace negative thoughts with positive ones, you'll start having positive results.

Willie Nelson

> Positive anything is better than negative nothing.

Elbert Hubbard

> Each day comes bearing its gifts. Untie the ribbon.

Ann Ruth Schabacker

> If you don't like the road you're walking, start paving another one.

Dolly Parton

> A dead end is just a good place to turn around.

Naomi Judd

> In every day, there are 1,440 minutes. That means we have 1,440 daily opportunities to make a positive impact.

Les Brown

> Friends are the family we choose.

Jennifer Aniston

"

My purpose: to lift your spirit and to motivate you.

Mavis Staples

❝

Kindness is one thing you can't give away. It always comes back.

George Skolsky

> Great things happen to those who don't stop believing, trying, learning, and being grateful.

Roy T. Bennett

> Try to be a rainbow in someone else's cloud.

Maya Angelou

> Sometimes, when things are falling apart, they may actually be falling into place.

Unknown

> Fight for the things that you care about, but do it in a way that will lead others to join you.

Ruth Bader Ginsburg

> Happiness is not by chance but by choice.

Jim Rohn

> "The greatest glory in living lies not in never failing, but in rising every time we fail.

Nelson Mandela

> Your attitude is critical to success. If you expect things to be difficult, it will always be easier to solve problems, overcome adversity, and have an enthusiastic

> You're going to go through tough times - that's life. But I say, 'Nothing happens to you, it happens for you.' See the positive in negative events.

Joel Osteen

> **Success is falling nine times and getting up ten.**

Jon Bon Jovi

> Don't waste a minute not being happy. If one window closes, run to the next window - or break down a door.

Brooke Shields

> The key to life when things get tough is to just keep moving. Just keep moving.

Tyler Perry

> Life's battles don't always go to the stronger or faster man. But sooner or later, the man who wins is the man who thinks he can.

Vince Lombardi

> Success is only meaningful and enjoyable if it feels like your own.

Michelle Obama

> Find out who you are and do it on purpose.

Dolly Parton

> Live life to the fullest, and focus on the positive.

Matt Cameron

> "
You'll never do a whole lot unless you're brave enough to try.

Dolly Parton

> Always turn a negative situation into a positive situation.

Michael Jordan

> Every strike brings me closer to a home run.

Babe Ruth

> Life is like a bicycle. To keep your balance, you must keep moving.

Albert Einstein

> Setting goals is the first step in turning the invisible into the visible.

Tony Robbins

> Know what sparks the light in you. Then use that light to illuminate the world.

Oprah Winfrey

> You only live once, but if you do it right, once is enough.

Mae West

> Be yourself, everyone else is already taken.

Oscar Wilde

> When I'm not feeling my best I ask myself, 'What are you gonna do about it?' I use the negativity to fuel the transformation into a better me.

Beyonce

> Believing you are unworthy of love and belonging - that who you are authentically is a sin or is wrong - is deadly. Who you are is beautiful and amazing.

Laverne Cox

> You can, you should, and if you're brave enough to start, you will.

Stephen King

> Speak your mind, even if your voice shakes.

Maggie Kuhn

> You're braver than you believe, and stronger than you seem, and smarter than you think.

A.A. Mine

> Perpetual optimism is a force multiplier.

Colin Powell

> Pessimism leads to weakness, optimism to power.

William James

> One of the things I learned the hard way was that it doesn't pay to get discouraged. Keeping busy and making optimism a way of life can restore your faith in yourself.

Lucille Ball

> Say something positive, and you'll see something positive.

Jim Thompson

> **Choose to be optimistic, it feels better.**

Dali Lama

> Optimism is a happiness magnet. If you stay positive good things and good people will be drawn to you.

Mary Lou Retton

> We cannot solve problems with the kind of thinking we employed when we came up with them.

Albert Einstein

> Learn as if you will live forever, live like you will die tomorrow.

Mahatma Gandhi

> Stay away from those people who try to disparage your ambitions. Small minds will always do that, but great minds will give you a feeling that you can become great too.

Mark Twain

> When you give joy to other people, you get more joy in return. You should give a good thought to the happiness that you can give out.

Eleanor Roosevelt

66

When you change your thoughts, remember to also change your world.

Norman Vincent Peale

> It is only when we take chances that our lives improve. The initial and the most difficult risk we need to take is to become honest.

Walter Anderson

> Nature has given us all the pieces required to achieve exceptional wellness and health, but has left it to us to put these pieces together.

Diane McLaren

> Success is not final; failure is not fatal: It is the courage to continue that counts.

Winston Churchill

> It is better to fail in originality than to succeed in imitation.

Herman Melville

> The road to success and the road to failure are almost exactly the same.

Colin R. Davis

> Success usually comes to those who are too busy to be looking for it.

Henry David Thoreau

> Develop success from failures. Discouragement and failure are two of the surest stepping stones to success.

Dale Carnegie

> Nothing in the world can take the place of persistence. Talent will not; nothing is more common than unsuccessful men with talent. Genius will not; unrewarded genius is almost a proverb. Education will not; the world is full of educated derelicts. The slogan 'Press On' has solved and always will solve the problems of the human race.

Calvin Coolidge

> There are three ways to ultimate success: The first way is to be kind. The second way is to be kind. The third way is to be kind.

Mister Rogers

> Success is peace of mind, which is a direct result of self-satisfaction in knowing you made the effort to become the best of which you are capable.

John Wooden

> I never dreamed about success. I worked for it.

Estée Lauder

> Success is getting what you want; happiness is wanting what you get.

W. P. Kinsella

> The pessimist sees difficulty in every opportunity. The optimist sees opportunity in every difficulty.

Winston Churchill

> Don't let yesterday take up too much of today.

Will Rogers

> You learn more from failure than from success. Don't let it stop you. Failure builds character.

Unknown

> If you are working on something that you really care about, you don't have to be pushed. The vision pulls you.

Steve Jobs

> Experience is a hard teacher because she gives the test first, the lesson afterward.

Vernon Sanders Law

> To know how much there is to know is the beginning of learning to live.

Dorothy West

> Goal setting is the secret to a compelling future.

Tony Robbins

> Concentrate all your thoughts upon the work in hand. The sun's rays do not burn until brought to a focus.

Alexander Graham Bell

> Either you run the day or the day runs you.

Jim Rohn

> I'm a great believer in luck, and I find the harder I work, the more I have of it.

Thomas Jefferson

> When we strive to become better than we are, everything around us becomes better too.

Paulo Coelho

> Opportunity is missed by most people because it is dressed in overalls and looks like work.

Thomas Edison

❝

Setting goals is the first step in turning the invisible into the visible.

Tony Robbins

> **Women challenge the status quo because we are never it.**

Cindy Gallop

> We don't just sit around and wait for other people. We just make, and we do.

Arlan Hamilton

> Think like a queen. A queen is not afraid to fail. Failure is another stepping stone to greatness.

Oprah Winfrey

"
The strongest actions for a woman is to love herself, be herself and shine amongst those who never believed she could.

Unknown

> Whenever you see a successful woman, look out for three men who are going out of their way to try to block her.

Yulia Tymoshenko

> Some women choose to follow men, and some choose to follow their dreams. If you're wondering which way to go, remember that your career will never wake up and tell you that it doesn't love you anymore.

Lady Gaga

"

The thing women have yet to learn is nobody gives you power. You just take it.

Roseanne Barr

> No woman wants to be in submission to a man who isn't in submission to God!

T. D. Jakes

> A witty woman is a treasure; a witty beauty is a power.

George Meredith

> When a woman becomes her own best friend, life is easier.

Diane Von Furstenberg

> If you want something said, ask a man; if you want something done, ask a woman.

Margaret Thatcher

> We need women at all levels, including the top, to change the dynamic, reshape the conversation, to make sure women's voices are heard and heeded, not

> It took me quite a long time to develop a voice, and now that I have it, I am not going to be silent.

Madeleine Albright

> Women must learn to play the game as men do.

Eleanor Roosevelt

> I swear, by my life and my love of it, that I will never live for the sake of another man, nor ask another man to live for mine.

Ayn Rand

> He who conquers himself is the mightiest warrior.

Confucius

> Try not to become a man of success, but rather become a man of value.

Albert Einstein

> One man with courage makes a majority.

Andrew Jackson

> One secret of success in life is for a man to be ready for his opportunity when it comes.

Benjamin Disraeli

> A man who has committed a mistake and doesn't correct it is committing another mistake.

Confucius Kongzi

> The successful man will profit from his mistakes and try again in a different way.

Dale Carnegie

> A successful man is one who can lay a firm foundation with the bricks others have thrown at him.

David Brinkley

> He is a wise man who does not grieve for the things which he has not, but rejoices for those which he has.

Epictetus

"

Even miracles take a little time

The Fairy Godmother, Cinderella

> Just keep swimming

Dory, Finding Nemo

> Those who don't believe in magic will never find it.

Roald Dahl, The Minpins

> It's a whole lot more satisfying to reach for the stars, even if you end up landing only on the moon.

Kermit the Frog, The Muppets

> Always let your conscience be your guide.

Jiminy Cricket, Pinocchio

> If it wasn't hard, everyone would do it. It's the hard that makes it great.

Tom Hanks

> You are braver than you believe, stronger than you seem, and smarter than you think.

A.A.Milne

"

The more that you read, the more things you will know. The more that you learn, the more places you'll go.

Dr. Seuss

66

First, think. Second, believe. Third, dream of coming true.

Walt Disney

> Somewhere inside all of us is the power to change the world.

Roald Dahl, Matilda

> You are your best thing.

Maya Angelou

> You've got to get up every morning with determination if you're going to go to bed with satisfaction.

George Lorimer

> Education is the most powerful weapon which you can use to change the world.

Nelson Mandela

> The most difficult thing is the decision to act; the rest is merely tenacity.

Amelia Earhart

> You'll find that education is just about the only thing lying around loose in this world, and it's about the only thing a fellow can have as much of as he's willing to haul away.

John Graham

> Take the attitude of a student, never be too big to ask questions, never know too much to learn something new.

Augustine Og Mandino

> It is remarkable how much long-term advantage people like us have gotten by trying to be consistently not stupid, instead of trying to be very intelligent.

Charlie Munger

❝

You can't be that kid standing at the top of the waterslide, overthinking it. You have to go down the chute.

Tina Fey

> When I believe in something, I'm like a dog with a bone.

Melissa McCarthy

> And the day came when the risk to remain tight in a bud was more painful than the risk it took to blossom.

Anaïs Nin

> The standard you walk past is the standard you accept.

David Hurley

> I've searched all the parks in all the cities and found no statues of committees.

Gilbert K. Chesterton

> Success is stumbling from failure to failure with no loss of enthusiasm.

Winston Churchill

66

Keep your eyes on the stars, and your feet on the ground.

Theodore Roosevelt

> Do not stop thinking of life as an adventure. You have no security unless you can live bravely, excitingly, imaginatively; unless you can choose a challenge instead of competence.

Eleanor Roosevelt

> Perfection is not attainable. But if we chase perfection we can catch excellence.

Vince Lombardi

> Get a good idea and stay with it. Dog it, and work at it until it's done right.

Walt Disney

> Optimism is the faith that leads to achievement. Nothing can be done without hope and confidence.

Helen Keller

> The elevator to success is out of order. You'll have to use the stairs, one step at a time.

Joe Girard

"

Be a positive energy trampoline - absorb what you need and rebound more back.

Dave Carolan

> People often say that motivation doesn't last. Well, neither does bathing - that's why we recommend it daily.

Zig Ziglar

> Work until your bank account looks like a phone number.

Unknown

> I am so clever that sometimes I don't understand a single word of what I am saying.

Oscar Wilde

> People say nothing is impossible, but I do nothing every day.

Winnie the Pooh

> Life is like a sewer ... what you get out of it depends on what you put into it.

Tom Lehrer

"

I always wanted to be somebody, but now I realize I should have been more specific.

Lily Tomlin

> Talent wins games, but teamwork and intelligence win championships.

Michael Jordan

> Individual commitment to a group effort - that is what makes a team work, a company work, a society work, a civilization work.

Vince Lombardi

> Teamwork is the ability to work together toward a common vision. The ability to direct individual accomplishments toward organizational objectives. It is the fuel that allows common people to attain uncommon results.

Andrew Carnegie

> Coming together is a beginning. Keeping together is progress. Working together is success.

Henry Ford

> Alone we can do so little, together we can do so much.

Helen Keller

> Remember, teamwork begins by building trust. And the only way to do that is to overcome our need for invulnerability.

Patrick Lencioni

66

I invite everyone to choose forgiveness rather than division, teamwork over personal ambition.

Jean-Francois Cope

> Just one small positive thought in the morning can change your whole day.

Dalai Lama

> Opportunities don't happen, you create them.

Chris Grosser

> Love your family, work super hard, live your passion.

Gary Vaynerchuk

> It is never too late to be what you might have been.

George Eliot

> Don't let someone else's opinion of you become your reality.

Les Brown

> If you're not positive energy, you're negative energy.

Mark Cuban

66

I am not a product of my circumstances. I am a product of my decisions.

Stephen R. Covey

> Do the best you can. No one can do more than that.

John Wooden

> # If you can dream it, you can do it.

Walt Disney

> Do what you can, with what you have, where you are.

Theodore Roosevelt

> "The greatest discovery of my generation is that a human being can alter his life by altering his attitudes.

William James

> One of the differences between some successful and unsuccessful people is that one group is full of doers, while the other is full of wishers.

Edmond Mbiaka

> I'd rather regret the things I've done than regret the things I haven't done.

Lucille Ball

> You cannot plow a field by turning it over in your mind. To begin, begin.

Gordon B. Hinckley.

> When you arise in the morning, think of what a privilege it is to be alive, to think, to enjoy, to love.

Marcus Aurelius

> # Mondays offer new beginnings 52 times a year!

David Dweck

> Be miserable. Or motivate yourself. Whatever has to be done, it's always your choice.

Wayne Dyer

> Your Monday morning thoughts set the tone for your whole week. See yourself getting stronger, and living a fulfilling, happier, and healthier life.

Germany Kent

> Friday sees more smiles than any other day of the workweek!

Kate Summers

> Oh! It's Friday again. Share the love that was missing during the week. In a worthy moment of peace and bliss.

S. O' Sade

> Every Friday, I like to high-five myself for getting through another week on little more than caffeine, willpower, and inappropriate humor.

Nanea Hoffman

> Make a Friday a day to celebrate work well done that you can be proud of, knowing that you just didn't put in time to the next paycheck.

Byron Pulsifer

> When you leave work on Friday, leave work. Don't let technology follow you throughout your weekend (answering text messages and emails). Take a break. You will be more refreshed to begin the workweek if you have had a break.

Catherine Pulsifer

"

You can get everything in life you want if you will just help enough other people get what they want.

Zig Ziglar

> Inspiration does exist, but it must find you working.

Pablo Picasso

> Don't settle for average. Bring your best to the moment. Then, whether it fails or succeeds, at least you know you gave all you had.

Angela Bassett

> Show up, show up, show up, and after a while the muse shows up, too.

Isabel Allende

> Don't bunt. Aim out of the ballpark. Aim for the company of immortals.

David Ogilvy

> I have stood on a mountain of no's for one yes.

Barbara Elaine Smith

> If you believe something needs to exist, if it's something you want to use yourself, don't let anyone ever stop you from doing it.

Tobias Lütke

> Life can be much broader once you discover one simple fact: Everything around you that you call life was made up by people that were no smarter than you. And you can change it, you can influence it. ... Once you learn that, you'll never be the same again.

Steve Jobs

> Life is like riding a bicycle. To keep your balance, you must keep moving.

Albert Einstein

> What you do speaks so loudly that I cannot hear what you say.

Ralph Waldo Emerson

> I have never let my schooling interfere with my education.

Mark Twain

> If you can't yet do great things, do small things in a great way.

Napoleon Hill

> If you really want to do something, you'll find a way. If you don't, you'll find an excuse.

Jim Rohn

> Be sure you put your feet in the right place, then stand firm.

Abraham Lincoln

> Live out of your imagination, not your history.

Stephen Covey

> Do not wait for the perfect time and place to enter, for you are already onstage.

Unknown

> The greater the difficulty, the more the glory in surmounting it.

Epicurus

> Courage doesn't always roar. Sometimes courage is a quiet voice at the end of the day saying, 'I will try again tomorrow.'

Mary Anne Radmacher

> If the decisions you make about where you invest your blood, sweat, and tears are not consistent with the person you aspire to be, you'll never become that person.

Clayton M. Christensen

"

Fear of what other people will think is the single most paralyzing dynamic in business and in life. The best moment of my life was the day I realized that I no longer give a damn what anybody thinks. That's enormously liberating and freeing, and it's the only way to live your life and do your business

Cindy Gallop

> The only way of discovering the limits of the possible is to venture a little way past them into the impossible.

Arthur C. Clarke

> Worry is a misuse of imagination.

Unknown

> Courage is the most important of all the virtues because, without courage, you can't practice any other virtue consistently.

Maya Angelou

> I never look back, darling. It distracts from the now.

Edna Mode

> A year from now you will wish you had started today.

Unknown

> The reason we struggle with insecurity is because we compare our behind the scenes with everyone else's highlight reel.

Steve Furtick

> Somewhere, something incredible is waiting to be known.

Carl Sagan

> I will not lose, for even in defeat, there's a valuable lesson learned, so it evens up for me.

Jay-Z

> I do not try to dance better than anyone else. I only try to dance better than myself.

Arianna Huffington

> If you don't risk anything, you risk even more.

Erica Jong

> Failure is simply the opportunity to begin again, this time more intelligently.

Henry Ford

> Our greatest glory is not in never falling, but in rising every time we fall.

Confucius

> If you change the way you look at things, the things you look at change.

Wayne Dyer

> We must reach out our hand in friendship and dignity, both to those who would befriend us and those who would be our enemy.

Arthur Ashe

> It's fine to celebrate success, but it is more important to heed the lessons of failure.

Bill Gates

> I can't tell you how many times I've been given a no, only to find that a better, brighter, bigger yes was right around the corner.

Arlan Hamilton

> We need to accept that we won't always make the right decisions, that we'll screw up royally sometimes- understanding that failure is not the opposite of success, it's part of success.

Ariana Huffington

> When everything seems to be going against you, remember that the airplane takes off against the wind, not with it.

Henry Ford

> You cannot always control what goes on outside. But you can always control what goes on inside.

Wayne Dyer

> We are what we repeatedly do. Excellence, then, is not an act, but a habit.

Aristotle

> Start where you are. Use what you have. Do what you can.

Arthur Ashe

> Hustle beats talent when talent doesn't hustle.

Ross Simmonds

> **Everything you've ever wanted is sitting on the other side of fear.**

George Addair

> The question isn't who is going to let me; it's who is going to stop me.

Ayn Rand

> Every strike brings me closer to the next home run.

Babe Ruth

> I have not failed. I've just found 10,000 ways that won't work.

Thomas Edison

❝
Don't worry about failure; you only have to be right once.

Drew Houston

> You carry the passport to your own happiness.

Diane Von Furstenberg

> Never let success get to your head, and never let failure get to your heart.

Drake

> Ideation without execution is delusion.

Robin Sharma

> Make sure your worst enemy doesn't live between your own two ears.

Laird Hamilton

> It is a rough road that leads to the heights of greatness.

Lucius Annaeus Seneca

> For the great doesn't happen through impulse alone, and is a succession of little things that are brought together.

Vincent Van Gogh

"
If we take care of the moments, the years will take care of themselves.

Maria Edgeworth

"

Resilience is when you address uncertainty with flexibility.

Unknown

> Sometimes magic is just someone spending more time on something than anyone else might reasonably expect.

Raymond Joseph Teller

> It's not the will to win that matters - everyone has that. It's the will to prepare to win that matters.

Paul Bryant

> As a single footstep will not make a path on the earth, so a single thought will not make a pathway in the mind. To make a deep physical path, we walk again and again. To make a deep mental path, we must think over and over the kind of thoughts we wish to dominate our lives.

Henry David Thoreau

> Never give up on a dream just because of the time it will take to accomplish it. The time will pass anyway.

Earl Nightingale

> True humility is not thinking less of yourself; it is thinking of yourself less.

Unknown

> The two most important days in your life are the day you're born and the day you find out why.

Mark Twain.

> Nothing ever goes away until it teaches us what we need to know.

Pema Chodron

> We can see through others only when we can see through ourselves.

Bruce Lee

> First, forget inspiration. Habit is more dependable. Habit will sustain you whether you're inspired or not. Habit will help you finish and polish your stories. Inspiration won't. Habit is persistence in practice.

Octavia Butler

> The best way out is always through.

Robert Frost

> The battles that count aren't the ones for gold medals. The struggles within yourself - the invisible, inevitable battles inside all of us - that's where it's at.

Jesse Owens

> If there is no struggle, there is no progress.

Frederick Douglass

> Someone will declare, 'I am the leader!' and expect everyone to get in line and follow him or her to the gates of heaven or hell. My experience is that it doesn't happen that way. Others follow you based on the quality of your actions rather than the magnitude of your declarations.

Bill Walsh

> Courage is like a muscle. We strengthen it by use.

Ruth Gordo

> Relentlessly prune bullshit, don't wait to do things that matter, and savor the time you have. That's what you do when life is short.

Paul Graham

> # More is lost by indecision than wrong decision.

Marcus Tullius Cicero

> If the highest aim of a captain were to preserve his ship, he would keep it in port forever.

Thomas Aquinas

> You can be the ripest, juiciest peach in the world, and there's still going to be somebody who hates peaches.

Dita Von Teese

> Keep a little fire burning; however small, however hidden.

Cormac McCarthy

> You'll never get bored when you try something new. There's really no limit to what you can do.

Dr. Seuss

> I think it's intoxicating when somebody is so unapologetically who they are.

Don Cheadle

> You can never leave footprints that last if you are always walking on tiptoe.

Leymah Gbowee

> If you don't like the road you're walking, start paving another one.

Dolly Parton

> If it makes you nervous, you're doing it right.

Childish Gambino

> What you do makes a difference, and you have to decide what kind of difference you want to make.

Jane Goodall

> I choose to make the rest of my life the best of my life.

Louise Hay

> In order to be irreplaceable one must always be different.

Coco Chanel

> Anything can make me stop and look and wonder, and sometimes learn.

Kurt Vonnegut

> People's passion and desire for authenticity is strong.

Constance Wu

> A surplus of effort could overcome a deficit of confidence.

Sonia Sotomayor

> Doubt is a killer. You just have to know who you are and what you stand for.

Jennifer Lopez

> No one changes the world who isn't obsessed.

Billie Jean King

> I learned a long time ago that there is something worse than missing the goal, and that's not pulling the trigger.

Mia Hamm

"

Some people want it to happen, some wish it would happen, others make it happen.

Michael Jordan